To the people of New York

OBERMANN
NEW YORK
MOMENTS

Foreword by Elliott Erwitt
Edited by Karsten Thormaehlen

Native New Yorkers are territorial, they seldom leave their own neighborhoods unless it is to go to a work place or an office or a bank. Occasionally the essential New Yorker will venture out to a trendy restaurant or to a baseball game or some event out of his sphere before directly returning home to his familiar surroundings. The classic New Yorker will rarely walk around just for the joy of seeing the diversity of the great melting pot that is his city.

It takes a hardy non-New Yorker to get to know the fundamental New York, its great and varied geography, its gestalt and its and many moods. It takes the adventurous curious foreigner to walk the streets in wonder at this marvelous multi-faceted city.

That New Yorker of this book is the essential Bernd Obermann who in magazine parlance would be described as a street man... as opposed to an indoor man. Fortunately for him, the street has always been the most interesting democratically available manifestation of a whole society that he now presents to us unvarnished.

Bernd Obermann lives modestly in the part of the city historically known as Hell's Kitchen, formerly a hot bed of the Mafia (as in the Godfather book and movie). He is intimately involved with his immediate surroundings, his bar, his laundry, his hang out, his grocery store. In his "day job" he works as a freelance photojournalist for any and all American and foreign publications. He is a seasoned craftsman who shoots and delivers whatever is required of him in his profession. But he has a private photographic life as well. In this volume you can see the result of it and of his curiosity and affection for his adopted city.

On occasion Bernd Obermann will lead groups of foreign tourists around the little known corners of the city as both a way of sharing his knowledge of the ins and outs of New York but also as a way of acquiring more knowledge that he then adds to his private work. He will lead his charges to undiscovered Harlem, Coney Island, the recently russianized Rockaways, to a new soul food restaurant, to the best pizza parlor in little Italy, to the best dim sum establishment in Chinatown, to the cheapest outlet store on a Sunday morning on Orchard street, to the best New York hot dog and pastrami sandwich at Katz's delicatessen, and on to the delights of Lebanese cooking in the bowels of the borough of Queens and so on and on. You really have to be a street man to know and be conversant with all this abundance.

There is no shortage of books about New York and most of them are descriptive while very few are interpretative and lived. With this "moments" book of Bernd Obermann you can walk along the streets with him and practically touch the gritty New York atmosphere.

Elliott Erwitt

Gebürtige New Yorker sind sehr ortsgebunden, sie verlassen selten ihre Nachbarschaft, es sei denn, um zur Arbeit, ins Büro oder zur Bank zu gehen. Gelegentlich wagt sich der echte New Yorker in ein angesagtes Restaurant, zu einem Baseball-Spiel oder einer anderen Veranstaltung außerhalb seiner Hemisphäre, bevor er auf direktem Wege nach Hause in seine gewohnte Umgebung zurückkehrt. Der klassische New Yorker wird kaum nur zum Spaß herumlaufen, um die Mannigfaltigkeit dieses Schmelztiegels, seiner Stadt, zu entdecken.

Man braucht schon einen unerschrockenen Nicht-New-Yorker, um das ursprüngliche New York kennen zu lernen: seine großartige, sich verändernde Geografie, seine Gestalt und vielfältigen Stimmungen; einen beherzten, neugierigen Fremden, der stets staunend die Straßen dieser wunderbaren, facettenreichen Metropole auf- und abläuft.

Dieser neugierige Alltagsabenteurer des vorliegenden Buchs ist Bernd Obermann, der in der Magazinsprache als „Streetman" bezeichnet werden würde... also ein direkter Gegensatz zum „Stubenhocker". Er hat sich seiner Wahlheimat New York mit den Augen eines Fotografens genähert, denn glücklicherweise war die Straße für ihn immer die interessanteste, demokratisch verfügbare Offenbarung einer ganzen Gesellschaft, die er uns ungeschminkt präsentiert.

Bernd Obermann lebt bescheiden in einem Stadtteil, der als Hell's Kitchen bekannt ist, früher ein heißes Pflaster der Mafia (wie im Buch und im Film „Der Pate" beschrieben). Er fühlt sich aufs Engste vertraut mit seiner unmittelbaren Umgebung, seiner Stammkneipe, seiner Reinigung, seinen „Hangouts", seinem Lebensmittelladen. In seinem Job arbeitet er als freier Bildjournalist für amerikanische und ausländische Publikationen. Er ist ein professioneller Fotograf, der alles, was auch immer von ihm in seinem Beruf verlangt wird, fotografiert und liefert. Aber er hat auch als Fotograf ein Privatleben. In diesem Bildband können Sie das Ergebnis seiner Neugier und Leidenschaft für New York bewundern.

Gelegentlich führt Bernd Obermann Gruppen ausländischer Touristen in weniger bekannte Ecken der Stadt, um sich einerseits über die In & Outs New Yorks mitzuteilen, aber auch, um sich andererseits neues Wissen anzueignen, das er dann in seine freien Arbeiten integriert. Diese Einsätze führen ihn ins unentdeckte Harlem, nach Coney Island, in das russische Viertel Rockaway, zu einem neuen Soulfood-Restaurant, zum besten Pizzabäcker Little Italys, zum berühmtesten Dim-Sum-Etablissement in Chinatown, zum billigsten Outlet-Laden an einem Sonntagmorgen auf der Orchard Street, zum bekanntesten New-York-Hot-Dog und Pastrami-Sandwich bei Katz's Delikatessen bis hin zu den Genüssen libanesischer Küche in Queens und so weiter und so weiter. Sie müssen wirklich ein „Streetman" sein, um das alles zu wissen und erleben zu können.

Eigentlich gibt es keinen wirklichen Mangel an New-York-Büchern, und die meisten sind eher oberflächlich, nur wenige sind interpretierend und tatsächlich „gelebt". Mit diesem Buch „New York Moments" können Sie mit Bernd Obermann durch die Straßen schlendern und das prickelnde New York Gefühl fast berühren.

Elliott Erwitt

Los neoyorquinos son territoriales, pocas veces salen de sus vecindarios a no ser que tengan que ir al trabajo, a una oficina determinada o a un banco. A veces, el neoyorquino corriente se aventurará fuera de sus límites para ir a un restaurante de moda, a un partido de béisbol u otro acontecimiento antes de regresar directamente a su entorno familiar. El clásico neoyorquino rara vez dará una vuelta por la mera satisfacción de contemplar ese gran crisol de la diversidad que es su ciudad.

A un extranjero le llevará un tiempo empezar a conocer el Nueva York básico, su grande y diversa geografía, su forma y sus muchos humores. El extranjero curioso y aventurero recorrerá asombrado las calles de esta maravillosa y polifacética ciudad.

El neoyorquino de este libro es el Bernd Obermann esencial, quien en el lenguaje de las revistas sería descrito como un hombre de la calle… en oposición al hombre de interior. Afortunadamente para él, la calle ha sido siempre la manifestación democrática a nuestro alcance más interesante de toda una sociedad, que ahora nos presenta en su estado puro.

Bernd Obermann vive de forma modesta en una zona de la ciudad conocida históricamente como Hell's Kitchen, anteriormente semillero de la mafia (como en el libro y la película de "El Padrino"). Está íntimamente comprometido con su entorno más cercano, su bar, su lavandería, su tienda de ultramarinos o los locales que más frecuenta. En su 'quehacer diario' trabaja de fotoperiodista freelance para cualquier publicación americana o extranjera. Es un artista experimentado que dispara y entrega todo lo que se le pide en su profesión. Pero también tiene una vida fotográfica privada. En este volumen puede verse el resultado de ello y de su curiosidad y cariño hacia la ciudad que ha adoptado.

De vez en cuando Bernd Obermann guiará a grupos de turistas extranjeros por los rincones menos conocidos de la ciudad tanto para compartir su conocimiento de los pormenores de Nueva York, como para adquirir más información que luego añadirá a su trabajo privado. Guiará a las masas al Harlem inexplorado, a Coney Island, a Rockaways, recientemente invadido por los rusos, a un nuevo restaurante afro-americano, al mejor establecimiento de dim sum de Chinatown o la mejor pizzería de Little Italy, al outlet más barato un domingo por la mañana en Orchard Street; desde el mejor perrito caliente de la ciudad o sándwich de pastrami en Katz´s Delicatessen, hasta las exquisiteces de la cocina libanesa en las entrañas del barrio de Queens, etc. Realmente hay que ser un hombre de la calle para conocer y estar familiarizado con todo esto.

Existen muchos libros sobre Nueva York, la mayoría de ellos son de tipo descriptivo y sólo muy pocos presentan un carácter interpretativo y actual. Con este libro de 'momentos' de Bernd Obermann uno puede recorrer las calles con él y casi tocar el ambiente enérgico de Nueva York.

Elliott Erwitt

Les New-Yorkais de souche ont un comportement territorial, c'est-à-dire que les rares fois où ils sortent de leur quartier, c'est pour se rendre sur leur lieu de travail, faire une démarche auprès d'une administration ou aller à la banque. Occasionnellement, le New-Yorkais bon teint s'aventurera hors de son secteur pour, par exemple, dîner dans un restaurant branché ou assister à un match de base-ball, avant de réintégrer directement son environnement familier. Le New-Yorkais type se promènera rarement pour le seul plaisir de voir la diversité du melting-pot qui est sa ville.

Il faut être un non-New-Yorkais bien trempé pour découvrir l'essence de New York, sa géographie vaste et multiple, sa physionomie et ses atmosphères diverses. Il faut être un étranger aventureux poussé par la curiosité pour arpenter les rues, ébloui par cette ville merveilleuse aux multiples facettes.

Le New-Yorkais de ce livre s'appelle Bernd Obermann, dont on dirait dans la langue des médias, que c'est un « homme des rues »... par opposition au casanier. Heureusement pour lui, la rue a toujours offert aux regards de tous la manifestation la plus intéressante qui soit d'une société dans son entier. C'est cette société qu'il nous présente sans fard dans cet ouvrage.

Bernd Obermann mène un train de vie modeste dans la partie de la ville connue sous le nom de Hell's Kitchen (« cuisine du diable »), autrefois aux mains de la mafia (comme dans le film adapté du roman Le Parrain). Obermann est parfaitement intégré dans son environnement immédiat: il évolue entre son bar, sa laverie, son lieu de prédilection et son épicerie. Il gagne sa vie comme photojournaliste freelance pour diverses publications américaines et étrangères.

C'est un homme du métier chevronné qui photographie le tout venant pour ses clients. Mais il photographie aussi à titre privé. Ce livre donne à voir le fruit de ce travail ainsi que sa curiosité et son affection pour sa ville d'adoption.

De temps en temps, Bernd Obermann accompagne aussi des groupes des touristes dans les endroits peu connus de la ville. C'est pour lui une manière de partager ses connaissances sur le New York secret, mais aussi une manière de faire de nouvelles découvertes dont il peut enrichir son travail personnel. Il emmène ses groupes dans le Harlem inconnu, dans Coney Island, dans le mini-Moscou des Rockaways, dans un nouveau restaurant de nourritures spirituelles, dans la meilleure pizzeria de Little Italy, ils leur montre les bonnes adresses de Chinatown, il leur fait découvrir un dimanche matin la boutique la moins chère d'Orchard Street, il leur fait manger le meilleur hot dog et le meilleur sandwich au pastrami de New York chez Katz's delicatessen et les initie aux délices de la cuisine libanaise dans les entrailles du Queens, pour ne citer que ces exemples. Il faut vraiment être un « homme des rues » pour connaître la ville aussi profondément.

Les ouvrages sur New York sont légion, mais la plupart d'entre eux sont descriptifs, et seul un petit nombre propose une lecture vivante de la ville. Moments de Bernd Obermann vous accompagnera dans vos promenades à travers la ville et vous plongera dans l'ambiance âpre de New York.

Elliott Erwitt

I newyorkesi doc si allontanano malvolentieri dal loro quartiere e se lo fanno è solo per andare a lavorare o per recarsi in qualche ufficio o in banca. Può capitare si avventurino in un qualche ristorantino "in" o a una partita di baseball oppure a qualche altra rappresentazione al di fuori del loro territorio abituale, ma tornano poi subito tra le mura domestiche. È raro trovare il classico newyorkese a passeggio per il solo gusto di godersi l'affascinante e vario spettacolo offerto dal grande crogiuolo che è la sua città.

Per conoscere New York veramente, la sua grandezza, la sua varietà territoriale e di atmosfere, ci vuole un forestiero risoluto e curioso che, pieno di stupore, si avventuri sulle strade di questa meravigliosa città dalle mille sfaccettature,

Il newyorkese "adottivo" che ci presenta questo libro è Bernd Obermann, un uomo della strada – per dirla nel gergo delle riviste – contrapposto al tipico "casalingo" newyorkese. Per sua fortuna, le strade sono un interessante palcoscenico esposto agli occhi di tutti e in cui si rappresenta un'intera società, rispecchiata a sua volta, senza fronzoli, nelle fotografie di Oberman.

Bernd Obermann vive senza grandi pretese in una parte della città conosciuta da sempre come "Hell's Kitchen", già covo di mafiosi (come nel "Padrino"). È strettamente legato al suo quartiere con il bar, la lavanderia, i ritrovi abituali, il negozio di alimentari. Di professione fa il fotografo freelance per riviste americane e straniere. È un professionista esperto in grado di fornire sempre il prodotto che gli viene richiesto. La fotografia, però, è una compagna altrettanto fedele della sua vita privata, ed è proprio questa che ritroviamo nelle pagine che seguono, come testimonianza della sua curiosità e dell'affetto per la città che l'ha adottato.

Ogni tanto Bernd Obermann fa da guida turistica e porta i visitatori negli angoli meno conosciuti della città. In questo modo non solo condivide le sue conoscenze sui retroscena di New York, ma coglie anche l'occasione per scoprirne sempre di nuovi con cui arricchire la sua attività fotografica. Porta quindi i suoi gruppi nella Harlem sconosciuta, a Coney Island, nelle Rockaway ormai in mano russa, nell'ultimissimo ristorante di soul food, nella migliore pizzeria di Little Italy o ad assaggiare i dim sum più autentici di Chinatown; la domenica mattina li condurrà a fare affari imbattibili all'outlet più economico di Orchard Street, da Katz dove si gustano i migliori hot dog e sandwich pastrami, oppure ancora ad assaporare le prelibatezze della cucina libanese nel cuore di Queens... Solo un vero "uomo della strada" può muoversi così a suo agio in questo paese di cuccagna.

Su New York non mancano certo i libri, ma la maggior parte di questi è descrittiva. Solo pochi interpretano veramente la città e la vivono. Grazie a questo libro di "momenti" colti da Bernd Obermann sembrerà quasi di passeggiare per le strade della città accanto a lui e di toccare con mano l'atmosfera sanguigna di questa metropoli.

Elliott Erwitt

NA REPUBLIC

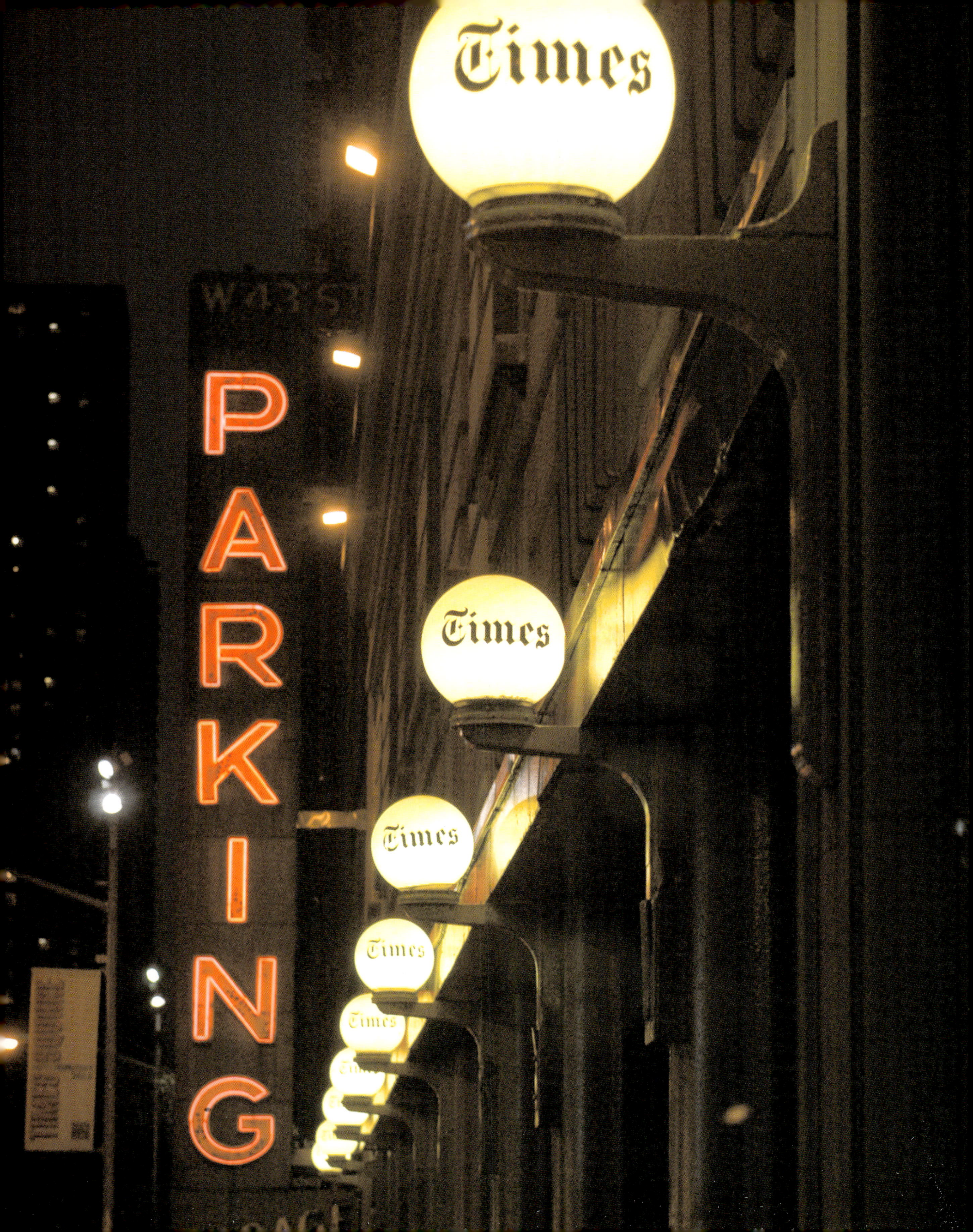
Times
W 43 St
PARKING
Times
Times
Times
Times

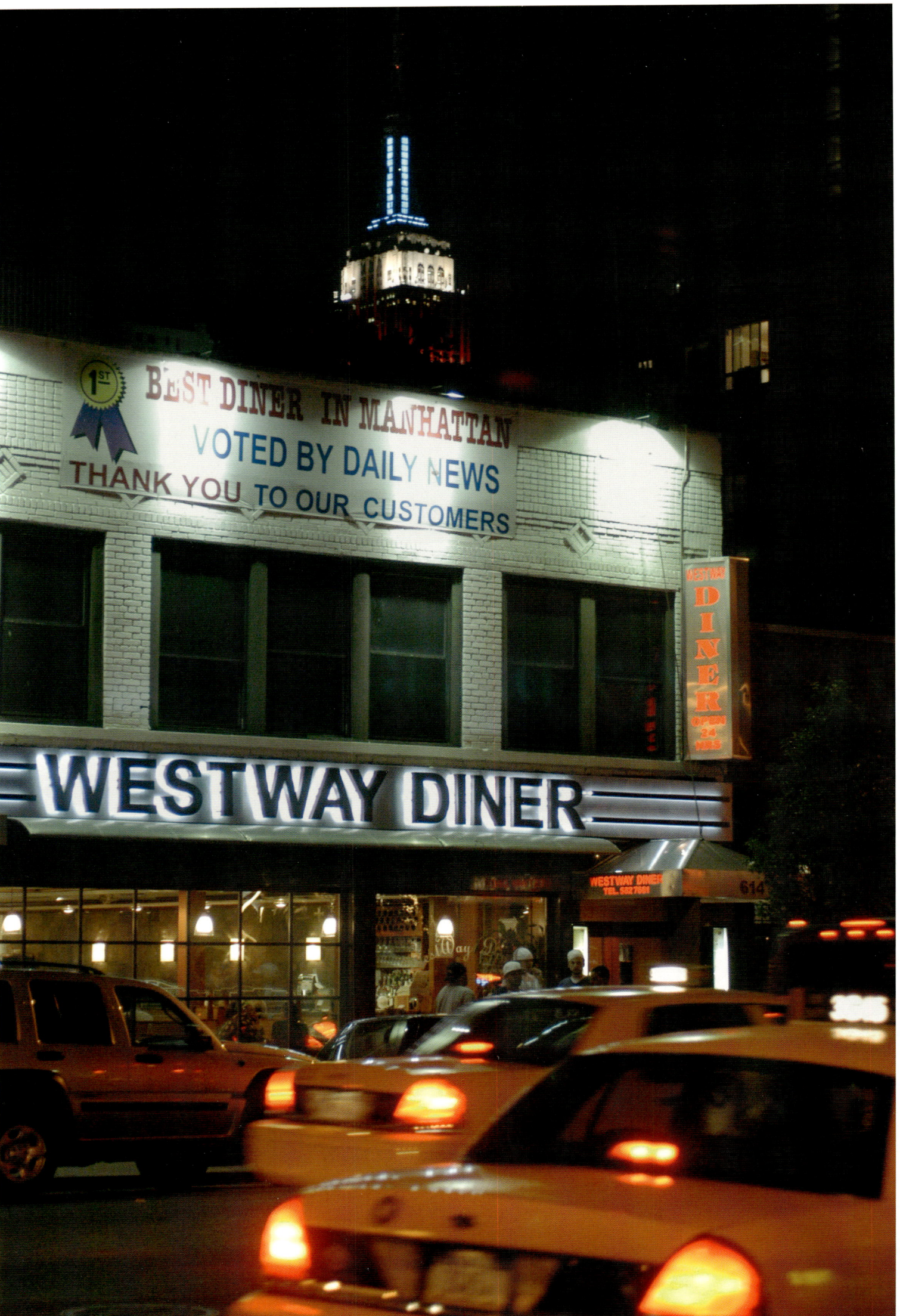

troCard is the
THE BIGGEST SHOW ON
42ND ST
M6
M7
M10
M16
M20
M27
M42
CLEARCHANNEL SPECTACOLOR

Biography

1954	born in Oberhausen, Germany
1971-1974	Apprenticeship under guidance of photographer Rudi Groth at the Head Office of Karstadt AG in Essen, Germany
1975-1976	Photo assistant of photographer Bernd Brenken, Paris, France and New York, U. S. A.
Since 1977	Freelance photographer for Bunte, Esquire, Focus, German Vogue, Ouick, Sipa, Stern, The New York Times, Die Welt, and many more
	Photo reports in Afghanistan, Canada, India, North Africa, Pakistan, Sarajevo, Somalia, Soviet Union, Spain, U. S. A, and other countries
Since 1996	he lives in New York

Bernd Obermann is contributing photographer at Corbis and at SLP Stock Photo Agency, which includes marketing arrangements with TimePix. He has already published two books about New York.

Acknowledgements

This book is dedicated to all the people who bought it.

Special thanks to Elliott Erwitt for his kindness to write the foreword
to my daughter Lena Obermann; I love to walk with her through this unique city.

Thanks to publisher Ralf Daab for his confidence and his support in my work,
to Karsten Thormaehlen and Feyyaz for the great design.
to Librado Romero, Head of Photography of The New York Times, for his help editing the photographs.
to my colleague Sebastian Kriete for his patience to teach me digital (photo-)technology,
to Volker and Nora Hanke for their friendship.

And last but not least all New Yorkers for their tolerance, which is for them not just a word
but a vital necessity.

© 2005 daab gmbh
cologne london new york

published and distributed worldwide by
daab gmbh
friesenstraße 50
d - 50670 cologne

p +49 - 221 - 94 10 740
f +49 - 221 - 94 10 741

mail@daab-online.de
www.daab-online.de

publisher ralf daab
rdaab@daab-online.de

art director feyyaz
mail@feyyaz.com

editing & layout karsten thormaehlen
mail@karstenthormaehlen.com

© photographs 2005 bernd obermann, new york
318 w 51st st
washington - jefferson - hotel
new york ny 10019 usa
p 212 246 7550
berndobermann@mac.com

represented by
polaris images
259 w 30th st
new york ny 10001 usa
p 212 967 5656
f 212 643 4544

© foreword 2005 elliott erwitt, new york

german translation karsten thormaehlen
spanish translation express translations gmbh
french translation christèle jany
italian translation raffaella durante-müller
copy editing bärbel philipp, dr. carmen garcía del carrizo

printed in spain
gràfiques ibèria, spain
www.grupgisa.com

isbn: 3 - 937718 - 43 - 5
d.l.: B-25563-2005